THE HOLY GRAIL

THE HOLY GRAIL

Sangeet Duchane

EVERGREEN

EVERGREEN is an imprint of
TASCHEN GmbH

© 2007 TASCHEN GmbH
Hohenzollernring 53, D-50672 Köln
www.taschen.com

© 2006 by Book Laboratory Inc.

Lay out: Kristen Garneau

Production English edition: Textcase, Hilversum, Netherlands
Typesetting cover for Textcase: Elixyz Desk Top Publishing, Groningen,
Netherlands

Printed in Singapore

ISBN-13: 978-3-8228-1664-6
ISBN-10: 3-8228-1664-7

Table of Contents

Introduction

The legend of the Holy Grail or Sangreal is over 800 years old and still has the power to capture our hearts and our imaginations. Today we find its themes and tales in books and movies and interwoven into popular culture. What is the magic of this story?

As we begin to look at the Grail legend, the first thing we notice is that there is not one legend, but several, with a lot of variation. We are going to retell two of those stories. The first formal Grail story, *Le Conte del Graal,* was written by Chrétien de Troyes in the twelfth century. About thirty years later a group of writers—many scholars think they were Cistercian monks—gathered and rewrote several Grail stories. Some of that material was later translated and modified by Sir Thomas Malory and published as *Le Mort D'Arthur.*

There are other versions of the tale that are familiar to us. The Bavarian knight Wolfram von Eschenbach wrote a story that formed the basis of Wagner's opera *Parsifal,* and Alfred Lord Tennyson wrote another version of the story.

What is the Grail?

The Grail itself is very different in these stories. Many people have come to think of the Grail as a cup or chalice that was used to catch the blood of Jesus as he died on the cross, but that was only one version. In the original story, the "Graal" referred to was not a cup, but a platter or serving dish. Other versions of the tale portray the Grail as the dish from which Jesus ate the Passover lamb at the last supper, the chalice of the first sacrament, the cup in which Joseph of Arimathea or Mary Magdalene caught the blood of Jesus as he hung on the cross or was taken down from the cross, a salver containing a man's head swimming in blood (as in the story of John the Baptist), a carved head of Jesus, the emerald that fell from Lucifer's crown as he plummeted to Hell, and a beatific vision.

Who Carries the Grail?

Sometimes a beautiful damsel or maiden carries the Grail, sometimes it floats through the air or on a beam of light on its own, and sometimes Joseph of Arimathea himself appears with it. It is often accompanied by a procession of young women, young men, or angels carrying candles, a lance, tables, and other ritual instruments.

The Grail in History

M ost of the early Grail legends were written between 1190 and 1240. To understand the Grail legend, it is important to understand what was happening during that time.

It was a time of excitement and religious fervor. Human life was cheap and easily lost, and a code of chivalry was developing that would help control the violence. Chivalry could be expressed by service to a king or a land, but it could also be expressed in some kind of religious quest.

New ideas about romance, about women, and about love were emerging. Out of this mix, a great legend was born and a quest was undertaken that has not ended to this day.

The Crusades to the Holy Land

T he first crusade to the Holy Lands was organized by Pope Urban II in 1095. The public reason for the crusade was a claim that the Turkish rulers in Jerusalem were attacking Christian pilgrims and desecrating Christian sites. The less public reasons were that the Turks were also threatening the Eastern Christian empire at Constantinople and that Europe had too many fighters with no one to fight. Calling for a popular crusade was the easiest way for Pope Urban to get public support for a war against the people called Saracens and perhaps mend fences with the Eastern Church as well.

The promoters of the Crusades portrayed the Muslims as barbarians; yet the culture of the Saracens, with its well-developed art, science, music, poetry, and philosophy, was far in advance of the European invaders. The Saracens had a level of culture that the Europeans would not reach until the Renaissance. The irony of the crusades is that they were responsible for bringing back this Islamic culture to parts of Europe never exposed to such ideas before. This Islamic culture may have included parts of the Grail stories, as we will see.

To promote the crusade, the Pope declared that all crusaders would receive forgiveness for all sins without penance, including those committed in the crusades, a guaranteed place in heaven, and all the riches they could plunder. With what could be interpreted as a license to rape, kill, and pillage, it is not surprising that the crusades included unconscionable brutality.

Against all odds the first crusade was a success, and Jerusalem was taken in 1100. The taking of Jerusalem was a bloodbath, in which the participants claimed to have killed residents of all ages without mercy. The Kingdom of Jerusalem was set up, with Godfrois de Bouillon as the first king of Jerusalem. The Holy Lands, or Levant, were divided into four states: Antioch, Edessa, Tripoli, and Jerusalem.

In 1146 Edessa fell to Saracens, and the second crusade was called to recover it. Pope Eugenius III put out the call, but the really impassioned pleas for war were made by the Pope's mentor, Bernard of Clairvaux. Bernard gave sermons in France and Germany, rousing the people to war. The effort, however, was a failure and ended with a failed siege of Edessa in 1148.

Jerusalem fell to the Saracens in 1187, and the third crusade was organized to reclaim it, but that effort failed as well.

At the beginning of the thirteenth century, Pope Innocent III called for a fourth crusade to recapture Jerusalem. Not enough money was raised to pay for a crusade, so the crusaders made a deal with the Venetians to pay for warships. The crusaders agreed to help the Venetians invade the Christian Byzantine Empire, and the crusaders eventually sacked Constantinople and killed many Eastern Christians. Pope Innocent temporarily excommunicated them for this, but when they brought back rich spoils to Europe, the excommunication was lifted. The crusaders were satisfied with the plunder of Constantinople, and Jerusalem was forgotten.

The Byzantine emperors had been collecting holy Christian relics for five centuries, and had amassed a very large collection. The invading European armies that sacked the city stole many of the relics. Some relics were lost, but many were brought back to Europe and formed the basis of pilgrim sites in the European Christendom of the following centuries.

The Order of Sion

The success in Jerusalem, short-lived though it was, had a major impact on Europe that lasted well beyond the kingdom of Jerusalem. One of the religious orders in Jerusalem was the Order of Sion, a group that some claim still exists today as a lay organization called the Priory of Sion. It is believed by some to be the guardian of the true Grail secret.

The *Ordre de Sion* was founded by Godfrois de Bouillon, the first King of Jerusalem, in 1190, ten years before the conquest of Jerusalem. Once Godfrois was king, he had an abbey built on Mount Sion in Jerusalem and gave it to the order. The Abbey is known in ancient documents as the Abbey of Notre Dame du Mount de Sion.

Some of the early members of the order were connected to Bernard of Clairvaux and the Count of Champagne.

The Knights Templar

and the Cistercians

The famous order of the Knights Templar was also founded in Jerusalem sometime after 1115. This order was formed by a group of men who had very close ties with Bernard of Clairvaux. Three of the Templar founders owed allegiance to the Count of Champagne, including the count's uncle who had close ties to Bernard. The count donated the property to Bernard where he built his successful monastery at Clairvaux. Bernard drafted the rule for the Templars and supported and promoted them after their foundation. In the two decades after the founding of the Templars, both the Knights Templar and the Cistercian order grew phenomenally, receiving many gifts of land and money.

The Knights Templar were soon the richest and most powerful religious order in Europe, and in 1139 the pope declared that the Templars answered only to the pope and were above the authority of civil rulers. The Templars consolidated their wealth and became the first European bankers who allowed travelers to deposit money in one place and draw it out at another Templar location.

The reason for the Templar's amazing growth and power has been one of the mysteries of history. One possible explanation for their power is that they, like others, collected relics, which were believed at the time to have benefi-

cial power, much like the Holy Grail. The Templars are said to have possessed the Shroud of Turin from 1207–1307, which might have given them status. People donating to the Templars could benefit from the power of the relics the Templars held. Some stories said that the Templars had a great treasure as well.

The Templars were housed by Baudouin I, the second king of Jerusalem, in the wing of the royal palace that had been built over the foundations of the Temple of Solomon. The Copper Scroll, an early Jewish document actually carved on thin sheets of copper, was found at Qumran as part of the Dead Sea scrolls. It lists various caches of Jewish buried treasure, and though it does not say where the treasure was buried, some think that part of it was buried under the Temple in Jerusalem. Many believe that the Templars excavated there and brought some of that treasure back to Europe. Others claim that the Templar treasure was one of knowledge, in the form of manuscripts.

The Templars were known for their fighting skills and were considered the best fighting force in the world at that time. Ironically, they also had quite good relations with the Saracens, their avowed enemies. They collected manuscripts and studied science, art, and philosophy. Carvings in their preceptories or monasteries showed they were familiar with astrology, alchemy, sacred geometry, numerology, and astronomy. They often had a good relationship with the Cathars of the Languedoc, who traded with the Saracens and were at peace with them. The Templars also had connections with several Jewish communities, including communities where the Kabbalah or Jewish mysticism was studied.

After the Saracens had retaken Jerusalem and other parts of the Middle East, the Templar role as a fighting force was outdated. They continued as financiers and political advisors, but not without making many enemies who resented their power and wealth. Their greatest enemy was Philippe IV of France. After some machinations, which probably involved the murder of at least one pope, Philippe managed to place his puppet, Clement V, in power in Avignon as the pope. In 1307 Clement and Philippe arranged for the arrest of all Knights Templar in France and the seizure of their property. The Templars who were taken in France were subjected to torture and imprisonment and many of them were burned alive. The Templars seemed to have had advanced warning of the arrest order, however, and a group of Templars escaped with the order's entire treasury. It is believed they went overland to the Templar ships at the north of France and sailed to a safe haven. Neither the Templar fleet nor the treasury appear in historical accounts again.

The Knights Templar are connected to the Grail story in more ways than their discovery of relics in the Holy Land. Wolfram von Eschenbach, one of the most prominent Grail writers, visited them in Jerusalem and made them the guardians of the Grail in his story *Parzival*. Several later writers also included the Templars in the Grail legend. Gahahad's shield in Le *Mort D'Arthur* is a Templar shield, though the story says that the red cross on the shield was drawn by Joseph of Arimathea in his own blood. This may be intended to indicate the high religious origins of the Templars, since Joseph of Arimathea is the great Christian messenger of that story.

The Cathars

A nother mysterious group of that era haunts us to this day: the Cathars of the Languedoc area of what is now France. They are usually called Gnostics, but the truth is that we know very little of what they taught or believed. It was the practice of the Church at that time to destroy the writings of anyone they considered "heretics," and the only information we have about several groups and individuals is what their opponents wrote against them. Much of what has been assumed about the Cathars is based on other so-called Gnostic groups such as the Arians, Marcionites, and Manichaeans.

The Cathars were a peaceful, non-violent people, living in a fertile area. Their culture was advanced, and they traded both goods and knowledge with the Saracens and Jews in the East as well as with their Western European neighbors. They studied the European languages and also Greek, Arabic, and Hebrew. They translated and studied Arabic manuscripts and had centers to study music, medicine, and philosophy that came from the East. There were schools of Kabbalistic study in Lunel and Norbonne. Their nobility, unlike most of their neighbors, was literate and educated.

The troubadours blossomed in their courts, and these same troubadours would carry the tales that became part of the Grail story around to the various courts of the Continent.

The religion of the Cathars was not an institutionalized church like the Western Christianity of the time, with doctrine and dogma. The Cathars believed in religious tolerance and allowed different points of view. They tended to believe in reincarnation, and recognized the feminine aspect of God. They rejected the idea of religious hierarchies and the concept of intercessors between humanity and God. Their preachers or teachers were both female and male, a fact that incensed the male clergy of the Church. The Cathars believed that knowing through their own understanding was more important than accepting secondhand knowledge or transmitted authority.

Cathars did not encourage procreation, though they were not against sexuality. Their *parfaits* or teachers took the sacrament of *Consolamentum*, in which they took a vow of celibacy, but that was usually when they were older and had lived a full life. Many only took the sacrament on their deathbeds. The Cathars were said to practice birth control, and perhaps abortion, which further infuriated the Church.

The Cathars were severe critics of financial corruption in the Church and of its violence. They did not spend money on churches, but worshiped out

of doors when possible or in any available building. They ate fish and vegetables, but no meat, and practiced meditation.

Needless to say, some of their neighbors were intrigued by them and became interested in their ideas. Their beliefs began to spread, which alarmed the Church. At one point Bernard of Clairvaux spoke against

them, but after he visited them, he found them to be pious people. Not so Dominic de Guzman, the founder of the Dominican order. He went to the Languedoc to convince the Cathars of their error. When he failed, he recommended using force to bring the Cathars into line with Church doctrine.

In 1208, a papal official was killed in the Languedoc, not by a Cathar, but allegedly by someone who supported the Cathars, the Count of Toulouse. That was enough for Pope Innocent III to call for another "crusade," which has come to be called the Albigensian Crusade.

The term crusade was a thin cover for systematic genocide, which the Church conducted for forty years until an entire people and an entire culture was destroyed. Once again, people of every gender and age group were slaughtered. Sometimes large groups were captured and then burned alive when they refused to renounce their faith. The Cathars were nearly wiped out, but there is a story that before the last stronghold at Montségur fell, four perfecti or parfaits escaped over the wall, taking with them the books and treasure of the Cathars.

The Knights Templar maintained an official neutrality in this war, though in practice the head of the order declared that there was only one crusade—against the Saracens—and Templars sometimes fought on the side of the Cathars.

The Courts of Love

One of the most remarkable people of this time was Eleanor of Aquitaine, heiress to a rich land and remarkable fortune. At 15 she married the king of France, Louis VII. Four years after their marriage, Bernard of Clairvaux began to preach in favor of the second crusade, which both Eleanor and Louis supported. Eleanor came to Bernard and pledged thousands of her vassals as crusaders. Bernard was probably a little less pleased about that when he discovered that she meant to go along with them. Eleanor, as many men would find throughout her life, was not easily dissuaded. She and 300 of her women and their servants joined the second crusade, purportedly to tend the wounded.

A dispute arose along the way between Louis and Eleanor's uncle Raymond. Louis wanted to head for Jerusalem and Raymond wanted to go directly to Edessa to take it back from the Saracens. Eleanor agreed with Raymond and when Louis insisted that she follow his orders, she publicly announced that their marriage was not legal because they were too closely related. Louis finally succeeded in forcing her to join his march to Jerusalem. When the eventual attack on Edessa failed, Eleanor and Louis returned to France on separate ships. Eleanor bore Louis two daughters before having the marriage annulled a few years later for the reason Eleanor had claimed earlier, that they were too closely related to legally marry. She left the children with Louis to be raised in the French court.

At 30 she married Henry of Anjou (though she was as closely related to him as to Louis), who was 11 years younger. Two years later he became king of England. She then spent many years giving birth to eight children, including her favorite, Richard the Lionhearted.

In about 1170 she set up her famous court at Poiters where the ways of courtly love were developed that would play such a large part in the Grail story. Like the Cathars, and despite her earlier fervor for crusade, Eleanor

had good relations with the Spanish Moors and gave patronage to poets, musicians, and troubadours. In her courts of love, she is said to have had women sit on a raised platform to judge the poetry in praise of women and other homage that the knights brought to them. Some historians dispute that story, but there is no doubt that Eleanor supported the development of the troubadours and their culture of courtly love.

This golden era did not last long, because in 1173 Eleanor convinced three of her sons to join her in a rebellion against Henry. The rebellion was defeated and Henry imprisoned Eleanor for fifteen years. On Henry's death, Eleanor's power rose again. She defended her son Richard's land while he was in the later crusades and raised money for his ransom when he was captured. She lived until her 80s and continued to wield political power and to arrange and influence marriages in the family.

Her work of courtly love was carried on by one of her daughters by Louis, Marie, Countess of Champagne. Marie was the patron of Chrétien de Troyes, the first Grail writer, who wrote some of his earlier work under her direction. He broke away from her direct influence, but there is no doubt that the concept of courtly love was an important part of the Grail story.

The Troubadours

The culture of the troubadours flourished in southern France from 1100 to 1300. The troubadours probably emerged from a tradition of nomadic entertainers called *histrions*, mimes, and *jongleurs*. The troubadours appear to have been from a higher social group than the others and were formally trained musicians, composers, and poets. It was a profession open to both women and men.

In the sixth century secular musicians had trouble with Church authorities, who said they were "responsible for infamous and diabolic songs of love." As a result, Caesar of Arles issued a decree banishing secular entertainers.

By the twelfth century secular performers were a deeply ingrained part of the culture and provided entertainment as well as preserving history for the wealthy elite. The troubadours had songs for every occasion: *sirventes* (political poems), *plancs* (dirges), *albas* (morning songs), *Jeux-patis* (disputes), and pastorals.

There were two languages of France at that time, *langue d'oc* in the south, largely spoken by the Cathers, and *langue d'oïl* in the north. The troubadours preferred the *langue d'oc*, since it was the more beautiful, but most songs had versions in both languages. Troubadour was actually the name for a southern musician. Their northern counterparts were originally called *trouvères*.

There is little doubt that the Arabic love poetry flourishing in the East at that time had a major impact on the development of ideas of courtly love. Some of the Provençal songs were translations from the Arabic, and Joseph Campbell believed that the word *troubadours* actually came from the Arabic root for music, and meant music maker or song maker.

Troubadours glorified nature and the senses. When the senses were ennobled and refined by courtesy, art, music, temperance, loyalty, and courage, they were reliable guides for the highest human realizations. Woman was to be respected, and no man could be a perfect knight if he did not love a woman. In a time when most marriages were formed for political or economic reasons, the troubadours sang of romantic love.

The troubadours had close ties with the Cathars and had many Cathar patrons. When the Cathars were attacked and their land taken, some troubadours were killed and imprisoned as well. Those who survived carried the Cathar culture with them into northern France and other parts of the Continent. The culture of courtly love and veneration of the Lady eventually moved into Great Britain, where it flourished.

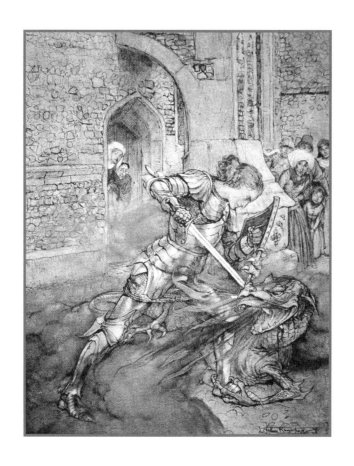

History in the Grail Legends

King Arthur and Britain

T he stories of the Grail legend usually take place in Britain and are placed in or around the court of King Arthur. One might wonder why the story of British history should flower in France as the Grail legends. The answer to that question is more clear if we look at the story of the historical Arthur and the Britons.

Our only record of a leader of the Britons named Arthur was written by a Welsh monk named Nennius around 830. He did not write a story of romance and magic, just a historical account of one of the last great leaders of the Britons, a story that is consistent with other historical accounts of the time.

The Romans conquered Britain in the first century B.C.E. and held it for about five hundred years, until the Visigoth attack on their empire required all their military strength back in Rome. In the absence of the Romans, Angles and Saxons from northern Germany were brought in to serve as mercenaries. Eventually the Anglo-Saxons became stronger than the original inhabitants and forced the native Britons south and east. In the late fifth century, archeological evidence shows that there was some reverse in this process, and the Britons made a stand and fortified a frontier. According to Nennius, the turning point was the Battle of Badon, dated elsewhere as 493 Nennius claims that the British warrior who led the Britons to victory was Arthur.

As a fifth-century leader Arthur would have been a Celtic warrior rather than a medieval king in armor, but the Grail writers just transplanted him into their own time. The castles of Tintagel and Winchester, which are connected to Arthur in legend, were actually built six centuries after the time of this Arthur.

According to archaeological evidence, one of the largest cities at the time of the Battle of Badon was Viroconium, near the border of Wales. It is one of the few Roman cities that was being rebuilt instead of falling into ruin during this period. This city had wooden buildings in a classical style, a drainage system, aqueducts, cobbled roads, and a large building that may have been a palace. This may have been Arthur's Camelot (a term not used until 1180 in Chrétien de Troyes' poem *Lancelot*).

The Celtic Arthur's kingdom did not hold out long against the Anglo-Saxons, and the Britons were eventually pushed into Wales and Brittany, taking their tales and their traditions with them.

Artifacts

There are several historical artifacts known at that time that might have had a great influence on the Grail stories. One such item was the Marian chalice. In the first part of the fourth century Constantine's mother Helena was in Jerusalem hunting for Christian sites from three centuries before. Since she was an empress, she tended to find what she was looking for, though

there is little historical information that would prove she found the right sites.

In 327 she ordered the excavation of what she believed to be the tomb of Jesus and found a chalice. A legend of the time said that Mary Magdalene had collected the blood of Jesus in the cup he used at the last supper, and Empress Helena believed the cup she found was that cup. It was called the Marian chalice, after Mary Magdalene. The story of Mary catching the blood at the foot of the cross is very similar to another legend that has survived in the Eastern Orthodox tradition. In that story, a woman standing at the foot of the cross, usually Mary Magdalene, is holding a basket of eggs which are stained red by the blood of Jesus. This is one of the stories told to explain why Easter eggs in many Eastern traditions are red. A twelfth-century icon shows the blood of Jesus pouring into the kind of jar Mary Magdalene is often pictured holding.

The Marian chalice was taken from Jerusalem to Rome, where it remained for a short time. The fifth-century historian Olympiodorus wrote that it was taken to Britain for protection in 410 when Rome was sacked by the Visigoths. It may have still been in Britain in Arthur's time some eighty years later.

There are different accounts about what the Marian Chalice actually was. Some say it was a small stone drinking vessel, some that it was a larger silver cup, and some that the original cup was incorporated by the Romans into a vessel with gold and jewels.

Another version of the Grail is a head of Jesus said to have been carved by Nicodemus. This idea may have been inspired by the *Volto Santo,* a carved image of Jesus on the cross that has been housed in the Lucca Cathedral in Tuscany since the twelfth century. This figure was believed to be the only true likeness of Jesus, and was said to have been carved by Nicodemus from his memory of Jesus. The carving attracted pilgrims from all over Europe in the Middle Ages.

Yet another Grail is an emerald. This may be connected to a relic stolen in the sack of Caesarea in 1101 that was carried to Genoa and is still in the cathedral there. This relic is a green glass dish, about 40 cm across that was once believed to be made of emerald. This relic, called the *Sacro Cantino,* was said to have been the gift of the Queen of Sheba to Solomon. In a thirteenth-century account by Archbishop Jacapo da Voraigre, he claims that is was the dish from which Jesus ate the last supper.

Two Grail Legends

Wₑ will now look at two of the most famous Grail legends and see how they are similar and how the tale changes over time. Even the spelling of character names changes, as Perceval becomes Percivale. The first tale, *Le Conte del Graal*, is a twelfth century tale by the Frenchman Chrétien de Troyes. This is an essentially Celtic tale. The second tale, *Le Mort D'Arthur*, by the Englishman Sir Thomas Malory was written about 300 years later and is an essentially Christian tale.

A Celtic Tale: The Quest of Perceval

C hrétien de Troyes' tale Le Conte del Graal contains many Welsh and Celtic elements. The story itself is similar to a purely Wesh tale called *Peredur*, that was written down by Lady Guest in her collection *Mabinogion* after Chrétien's story was written. There is little doubt, however, that *Peredur* is the older story and forms part of the basis for Chrétien's version. There are also elements of the Celtic tale of Kulhwah and Olwen that dates almost a century earlier than Chrétien's tale.

Some commentators believe that two of the women in this story, the Grail maiden and the Loathly Damsel, are two aspects of the Sovranty of Ireland. She was a Goddess who appeared both as a beautiful young woman and as an ugly hag. There is also a Celtic tale of Erris, an enchanted isle with a castle that was visible only every seven years, when the king came to the mainland. If a person meeting him asked the right question, the king would tell the person where heaps of gold were located and the enchantment of the king and the island would be removed. This sounds very much like the Grail castle that is hard to find and where a visitor must ask the right question to remove the enchantment.

The Fisher King in Chrétien's story resembles the Welsh character Bran the Blessed. Chrétien's Fisher King is wounded in the thigh (which may mean genitals) or leg with a javelin, and Bran is called "The Pierced Thigh." The horn of Bran provided unlimited food and drink for people, as does the Grail that is in the keeping of the Fisher King.

Chrétien's Grail also resembles several magical cauldrons of Celtic tales. Those cauldrons could provide food and drink, though they would sometimes only do so for the worthy, and they could also bring the dead back to life if the bodies of the dead were dipped into the cauldrons.

The focus of Celtic tales is on the virility of the king that is needed to provide sovereignty of the land. The king's sexual virility was necessary to guarantee the fertility of the land and the safety of the people. Some of the ancient Celtic rituals for crowning the king required him to demonstrate his virility before he was crowned. The land, seen as female, was the mate of the king.

If Chrétien's Fisher King was actually wounded in his genitals, as many believe, and was impotent, then the land would suffer. In this story we find that not only is the king in great pain, but the land is laid waste and the maidens are to be left without protection unless the king is healed.

Chrétien himself claimed that he got the story from his patron, Philip, Count of Flanders, a renowned crusader. Wolfram von Eschenbach claimed that the story was an Arabic tale from the Middle East that he obtained in Spain, and that Chrétien had told it wrong. It is possible, therefore, that this first Grail story is a combination of Celtic tales brought to Brittany by the fleeing Britons, and a story from the Arabic Middle East.

Le Conte del Graal

I n this tale Perceval's father, Bliocadron, was one of twelve brothers who were all killed in battle or in tournaments. Bliocadron was a king, but his land had been stolen by two knights. Bliocadron's wife, tired of all the carnage and fearing for the life of her only son, took him to live deep in a forest. She intentionally left Perceval ignorant about chivalry and knights, telling him that if he saw men who looked as though they were carved in iron, they were devils and he should run away.

All of her efforts were to no avail, however. When Perceval saw knights in the forest he thought they were angels. They explained they were knights, and Perceval was immediately determined to be one too. His mother could not talk him out of going, so she dressed him in fool's clothing, hoping he would be laughed at and come back home. She gave him advice about women he might meet, telling him that he should only take a kiss and a token from them, such as a ring or trinket.

She tried to talk to Perceval about religion, but he became impatient and left her in a swoon of grief, without looking back. He came upon a fine tent with a woman sleeping. He kissed the woman against her will, took her jewelry, and then helped himself to food. He did not listen to anything she said to him, and left her to face her husband, who accused her of being unfaithful when he found her jewelry gone.

Perceval rode on to the court of King Arthur, and nearby he met a knight in beautiful red armor, which Perceval desired. The knight had taken a cup from King Arthur's table because of some dispute about land. In the process he had spilled wine on the queen. The knight told Perceval to take a message to the king and to say that the king was to send a champion to fight for the cup.

None of the knights in the court wanted to challenge the Red Knight, and Perceval asked Arthur to give the armor to him. Sir Kai, Arthur's seneschal, mocked Perceval by telling him that Arthur agreed.

A fool of the court had prophesied that a certain lady would not laugh again until she saw the greatest knight. Through several tournaments she had not laughed, but as Perceval walked out in his fool's clothes, she laughed without thinking. Sir Kai was furious, slapping her and beating the fool who had made the prediction. Perceval was upset that he had caused trouble to the lady.

He rode out to the Red Knight and arrogantly demanded the armor. The Red Knight sneered and hit Perceval with the butt of his lance, but Perceval threw a javelin through the Red Knight's visor into his eye, killing him. Perceval began to pull at the armor, caring little for the knight. He could not manage the armor until a page from the castle came to help him. Perceval refused to take off the clothes his mother had given him, and put the armor on over them.

Perceval sent the page back to the court with the cup and vowed not to return to the court until he had avenged the lady who was slapped because of him. Perceval came to the castle of Gurnemanz of Gohart, who taught him the skills of a knight. Guremanz also gave Perceval a new set of advice. He should be merciful to knights he has vanquished, avoid being too talkative, help anyone in distress, and attend church.

Gurnemanz offered Perceval his daughter's hand, but Perceval was determined to have more adventures. He came to a castle of an old, lame king, who turned out to be one of his mother's brothers. Perceval sat by the fire with this king and watched two youths in a mock battle. Perceval fought the best of them, and the king said that Perceval would be the greatest knight. He must drop his mother's teachings and adopt a male code of honor.

Perceval moved on and came upon another castle belonging to another maternal uncle. In his sword practice he struck a metal column three times and broke his sword each time. Two times he was able to mend his blade, but not the third. His uncle told him that he had only come into two-thirds of his strength.

Next, Perceval came upon a castle under siege, where the people were starving. The beautiful queen, Blancheflor, had refused to marry the invader Clamadeu. Perceval offered to fight him for her if she would marry him. Blanceflor offered to marry him anyway, but he was determined to fight. On the next day Perceval defeated the

senechal of Clamadeu and on the day after he defeated two knights. That night a ship wrecked in the harbor and the people had food. The next day Perceval defeated Clamadeu and sent him to Arthur's court to serve the lady who was slapped, where he had already sent Clamadeu's seneschal. With peace restored to the city, Perceval and Blanceflor married.

They lived happily together for some time, but Perceval began to worry about his mother and wanted to see her again. He set out to find her and met a fisherman and asked him where he could lodge for the night. He was directed to a castle, where he discovered that the host was one of the fishers in the boat. This man was leaning on his elbow before a great fire. Perceval was curious about why he did not stand, but remembering the advice of Gurnemanz that he should not be too talkative, Perceval did not ask.

A boy entered with a sword, saying that it had come from the king's niece. The sword could not be broken except at one perilous moment that only the forger of the blade knew about. The king gave the sword to Perceval, saying he was destined to wear it.

Another youth entered carrying a lance that was dripping blood from the tip. Two more youths brought in candelabras, and a fair maiden entered with a jeweled, golden vessel—the Grail. The maiden and the Grail gave off a light that dimmed the candles. Another maiden came in with a silver dish. Perceval was curious, but he did not ask whom the grail served or the meaning of the procession. He put the questions off until the morning for fear of offending.

He woke in the morning to an empty castle, and when he rode out the drawbridge, he had to jump off the end when it was pulled up abruptly. Perceval came upon a maiden grieving over her dead lover who had just been slain by a knight. The maiden was Perceval's cousin. When she asked his name he said, Perceval of Wales, though he did not know his name before.

She called him Perceval the Wretched and explained that if he had asked the questions he was wondering about at the castle, the king would have been healed and would have been able to rule his lands. Perceval had made this error, she explained, because he had wronged his mother, who died from grief after he left her so heartlessly. As a result of this, the sword Perceval has been given would fail him at his greatest need.

Perceval went off to find the knight who had killed his cousin's lover, but met instead a wretched woman on an old nag. She was the woman Perceval had taken the jewelry from on the day he left his mother, and her husband had disgraced her. Perceval defeated the husband in a fight and then reunited them and sent them to Arthur's court.

Arthur was intrigued by this knight who kept sending so many knights to the court, and he set off with a hunting party to find him. As Perceval was riding near their camp, a falcon attacked a goose, which escaped after leaving three drops of blood on the snow. Perceval was mesmerized by the three drops, which reminded him of his wife's lips and rosy cheeks against her fair skin. While Perceval was in this trance, one of Arthur's knights came upon him and challenged him. Perceval defeated him without waking up. Next, Sir Kai challenged him, and Perceval unhorsed him, breaking his shoulder.

Gawain greeted Perceval just as the snow was melting, and Perceval came out of his trance. When Perceval was brought into the camp, Arthur and the company had a celebration, until the Loathy Hag, a hog-faced woman, rode up on a mule. She upbraided Perceval for not asking the questions at the Grail castle and healing the Fisher King. Because the king could not rule the land, the women would lose their husbands, the land would be waste, and the maidens would be left as orphans and helpless.

The Loathy Hag then announced some adventures: a joust and a maiden in distress. Gawain chose to help the maiden, while the others headed for the joust. Perceval vowed not to spend two nights in the same place until he discovered the answers to the two questions he failed to ask. Who was served from the Grail? What was the truth of the bleeding Lance?

Gawain was falsely accused of murder and arranged to meet for a fight to settle the accusation. In the meantime he set out on adventures and served as the champion for two younger daughters, winning the day. He met a woman and fell in love, but the man who had accused him of murder incited the people against the lovers and they were

forced to defend themselves using a chessboard as a shield, huge chess pieces, and the sword Escalibord. The king came to stop the fight and postponed Gawain's fight with his accuser for one year, on the condition that Gawain go in search of the Lance at the Grail Castle.

Meanwhile, Perceval had been wandering around for five years without entering a church. He was criticized by penitents for wearing armor on Good Friday, and then met a hermit whom he asked for advice. The hermit told him that his suffering was caused by his mother's death and that it was sin that stopped him from asking the questions about the Grail.

Gawain met a woman under a tree near a fountain and accepted her offer to accompany him, though he was warned against her. They were followed by a rude dwarf who continually insulted Gawain. When Gawain's horse was stolen he had to ride the dwarf's old nag and bear ridicule from the woman. In spite of it all, he remained chivalrous to her.

Gawain caught up with the knight who had his horse, defeated him, and reclaimed the horse. A ferryman wanted the horse as a toll, but Gawain gave him the defeated knight instead. The ferryman warned Gawain that the Castle of Marvels where he was going was haunted, but Gawain went on.

In the castle he was given the Perilous Bed to sleep in, and in the night he was assaulted by 700 bolts and arrows and had to kill a ravenous lion. He survived the challenges and the enchantment of the castle ended. He found that the three queens who had been held prisoner were his grandmother, mother, and sister. He became king of the castle and won the woman from the fountain.

Here the story ends, because Chrétien had not finished it when he died. We are left without a resolution of Perceval's story. Did Perceval find the Grail castle again? When did the sword fail him? Several other writers finished the story for Chrétien de Troyes. In some, Perceval finally completed the Grail quest. In others, Perceval failed and Gawain became the Grail hero.

A Christian Tale: The Quest of Galahad

y the time Sir Thomas Malory's translation of the earlier French tales of Arthur and the Grail were written in English in 1470, the story had become a thoroughly Christian tale, though, as we shall see, a somewhat heretical one. In this story priests and religious hermits play a much bigger role. They interpret the events of the story according to Christian doctrine, and sin is couched in terms of sexuality. The most important thing about Galahad is that he has never had sex. It does not matter that he kills quite a few people before the end of the story.

The story of the Grail is no longer a story about sovereignty of the land. It is a tale about mystical union and repentance for sin. Perceval was a very flawed youth who went on a journey of growth and development. Galahad is a Christ figure who casts out demons and saves souls from fire. He is good—the greatest knight in the world—

from the very beginning. Percivale, Bors, and Lancelot, the secondary achievers of the Grail, are the flawed human figures who must be saved by the grace of God.

The "old law," or Celtic way of life, is equated with the devil on more than one occasion. The devil also often takes the form of a seductive woman. Only the law of Christianity is good. Women play a lesser role in this story. The Grail is no longer carried by a maiden, but is usually held by Joseph of Arimathea. The other maidens in the Grail procession have been replaced by angels.

This is not orthodox Christianity, however. Galahad's search for mystical union takes place outside the Church, and is in the form of visions, which were suspect in the Church. Percivale's sister is also a Christ figure, who dies to save another and whose body gives off an aura of sweetness. Those around her are fed on manna from heaven. She seems to have no need to achieve the Grail. The main Christian apostle who is the source of authority for this story is Joseph of Arimathea, who some legends say brought the Grail cup to England after the crucifixion. Galahad is a Christ-like figure because he is a descendent of Joseph. The apostolic succession in this story seems to begin with Joseph, instead of with Peter, which was contrary to the teachings of the Roman Church.

Malory wrote this story from prison, where he spent a significant part of his life. He was originally imprisoned for a variety of crimes from adultery to theft, but the most important part of his offense seems to have been attacks against the Lancastrians

during the civil war known as the War of the Roses. Malory was released when the Yorkists came to power, but then changed sides and was imprisoned as a Lancastrian.

Malory said that he wrote with the aid of "certain French books" written 300 years before. Malory not only borrowed the basic story from these texts, but he also improved the storytelling style and created a classic tale. The Quest for the Holy Grail begins in Book 13 of Malory's tale.

Le Mort D'Arthur

T he company of the Round Table were gathered in preparation for the feast of Pentecost, when a gentlewoman came in and asked for Lancelot to come with her. She promised that he would be back in time to celebrate the feast.

She took Lancelot to an abbey where he found two Knights of the Round Table sleeping. Twelve nuns brought out Galahad. (We know, though Lancelot does not, that Galahad is Lancelot's son by Lady Elaine, the daughter of King Pelles, the lord of the Grail castle. Lancelot slept with Elaine because he was magically made to think that she was Queen Guenever, his beloved. Elaine and Pelles knew that Galahad, the one most worthy of the Grail, would be born as a result of that night's union.)

Galahad asked Lancelot to make him a knight and Lancelot agreed. Lancelot and the other two knights returned to the castle, but Galahad said he would follow later. The next day the company of the Round Table went to Mass to celebrate the feast day, and when they returned to the Round Table, they found that every seat or siege had a name on it, except for the Siege Perilous, where no one could sit. On that seat was written that 453 years after the passion of Jesus the seat would be occupied. Lancelot calculated that the seat should be occupied that very day.

A squire came to inform the King that there was a stone with a sword in it floating in the nearby river. The company went out to see, and found a message that only the best knight in the world could draw the sword out. Arthur encouraged Lancelot to draw it, but Lancelot knew he was not the best knight in the world. He refused and warned the others that if someone attempted to draw the sword and failed, the sword would give him a terrible wound at some time in the future. In spite of this warning Arthur insisted that first Gawain and then Percivale try to draw the sword. Both of them failed, and the company returned to the Round Table for its dinner.

The Siege Perilous was empty and had been covered with a cloth. An old man came in with Galahad, saying that Galahad was from the King's lineage and kindred to Joseph of Arimathea. He pulled back the cloth on the Siege Perilous, revealing Galahad's name, and Galahad took his seat.

After the feast Galahad pulled the sword from the stone in the river, saying that it was the sword that gave his grandfather Pelles a wound that only he could heal. As Arthur and the Knights were standing by the river, a lady in white came down it and told Lancelot that the company would be served by the Grail.

Arthur realized that the Knights of the Round Table were going on the Grail Quest and that the Quest would break up the Round Table forever. He scheduled one last joust so that the Knights could be remembered. Afterward they sat down at the Round Table for a feast and the Grail appeared to serve them with whatever they desired, but

it was covered in white samite (silk). They could not see the Grail or the person carrying it.

Gawain declared that he would go on a Quest to find the Grail and others joined in. Arthur and Guenever lamented the ending of the Round Table, but the next day 150 Knights set off on the Quest.

Galahad rode off without a shield, because he had not yet found the one he was supposed to have. He came to an abbey where a shield was hanging that only the best knight in the world could take. If the wrong person took it, that person would be killed or maimed within three days. Bademagus had arrived before Galahad and decided to take the shield. He did not even ride two miles before he was confronted by a white knight who told him to return the shield to Galahad. The shield was white with a red cross that the white knight said was drawn by Joseph of Arimathea in his own blood. The shield was intended for Joseph's last descendent, Galahad.

At the abbey Galahad was taken to a tomb where the monks heard terrible noises. Galahad opened the tomb and found a fiend. The fiend fled in fear, and Galahad ordered the body taken out of hallowed ground, since the man was evil. A priest came and told Galahad that the wicked man represented all the sin found in the world.

Galahad then rode to the Castle of the Maidens to destroy a wicked custom there. He was warned to stay away, but he was determined. He defeated seven evil knights and freed the castle. The priest came again and told Galahad that the good people who

lived in the castle before were the good people who lived before Jesus and the seven wicked knights were the seven deadly sins. Just as Jesus had delivered the souls of good people from hell, Galahad delivered the maidens of the castle from the wicked knights.

Next Galahad fought with Lancelot and Percivale, who did not recognize him. He outfought them, and a hermit came out of her hut and hailed him as the best knight in the world.

Lancelot

Lancelot rode on alone into the forest, where he came to a ruined church with a fair altar. He tried to go into the chapel to the altar, but it was closed to him. He set his horse to graze, took off his helmet and sword, and fell asleep. While he slept a wounded knight came to be healed by the Grail. Lancelot perceived part of this in his dream, but he could not move or wake. When he left, the knight took Lancelot's horse, helmet, and sword.

Lancelot awakened to the realization that he had proved unworthy and was wretched. When he realized that his horse and weapons were gone, he believed that God was displeased with him. He went on foot to a hermit who explained his sins to him and he repented.

Percivale

Percivale kept looking for the knight with a white shield, since he did not yet realize the knight was Galahad. Instead he met a hermit who was his aunt. She told him that his mother was dead of sorrow because he left her. She also told him that the knight he was seeking won through a miraculous power and would never be overcome by a man's hand.

Percivale then came to a monastery where he found an old king with many wounds. A brother explained to Percivale that this was a king who came to Britain with Joseph of Arimathea and had become so greedy for the Grail that it struck him almost blind. He repented and asked not to die until he could see and kiss his descendent who would achieve the Sangreal. The old man kissed Percivale and his sight was restored, even though he was over 300 years old.

As Percivale rode away from the monastery he was attacked by 20 men and was in trouble, until Galahad rode up to save him. Though Galahad rode away before Percivale could thank him, Percivale realized who he was.

Percivale had lost his horse in the battle, and a yeoman loaned him a hackney to ride to recover it. When he caught up to the knight who had taken the horse, the knight refused to fight, killed the hackney instead, and rode off with Percivale's horse. Percivale was furious and disgusted at this lack of chivalry and honor and, throwing his sword aside, he lay down to sleep.

He woke to find a woman before him who asked him what he was doing. When he explained, she said that if he would do what she asked she would loan him her horse. He agreed, and she brought an incredible black horse. Percivale rode until he came to some dangerous water. The horse wanted to ride into the water, but as Percivale pulled the horse back he made a sign of the cross on his forehead. The horse suddenly threw him off and dashed into the water. Percivale realized that the horse was a fiend meant to destroy him.

Percivale was lost in the wilderness without a horse, and he prayed for protection. He saw a huge serpent carrying a young lion in its mouth being stalked by an older lion. Percivale killed the serpent and the lion befriended him. As they slept together, Percivale dreamed of two women: one riding a serpent and one riding a lion. One of the women told him that he would have to fight the strongest champion the next day.

The serpent woman complained that he had killed her serpent. She wanted Percivale to be hers, but he refused. He woke in the morning feeling weak, and saw a ship coming. On it was a man dressed as a priest. The man said he had come to comfort Percivale. He explained that the lion was the new law of the Church, and the serpent was the old law and a fiend. He then left.

Another ship came in covered in black silk. A beautiful woman was on board and told him that the man who had just come was an enchanter, and he should not listen to him. She had been disinherited by a man and asked for Percivale's help to get her property back. Percivale agreed.

When they ate, Percivale ate and drank too much. He fell in love with the woman and vowed to be her servant. He was about to get into bed with her, when he saw the cross of his sword hilt and made the sign of the cross. The pavilion turned upside down and everything dissolved into smoke. Percivale realized that he had fallen for another demon, and stabbed himself in the thigh as penance. The man in the ship returned and told him that the woman was the devil, the woman riding a serpent. She would have defeated him except for the grace of God.

Lancelot

The hermit Lancelot had been staying with gave him a horse, helmet, and sword and he rode on. He came to a chapel where a very old man was lying dead and the priest was worried about whether he died in grace. The man had taken religious vows, but was wearing secular clothes. The priest conjured up a demon to tell him how the man had died. The demon told him that the man died in grace and that his clothing had been changed by others.

Then the priest turned his attention to Lancelot and told him that if he found the Grail, he would not be able to see it because of his sin. Lancelot wept. The priest told him to take the dead man's hair and wear it next to his skin and to eat no flesh and drink no wine while he was on the Quest.

On his way again, Lancelot met a woman on a white palfrey, who told him he would soon be easy about that which he was then in doubt. He came to a cross, and before sleeping he prayed that he would never fall into deadly sin again. He dreamed about kings and knights coming to the Grail for their reward. One was refused as unworthy.

Lancelot met the knight who took his horse. He knocked the knight off his horse and took it, leaving the other. He met a hermit and told him the dream. The hermit said that the people in the dream were the kings converted by Joseph of Arimathea and Galahad. He told Lancelot that Galahad was his son.

Lancelot was pricked by the hair in his shirt, but he bore it. He came to a castle where a battle was being fought, white against black. Lancelot joined the black side and fought until he was exhausted. He was led into the forest where he fainted. Lancelot was shamed by losing the battle and dreamed of an old man who asked him why he is turned toward sin. When he woke up, Lancelot went to an anchorite who lived in the wall of a church and asked her the meaning of his dream. She explained that the black knights in the battle were sinful and the white were chaste. Lancelot was so weak that he could not see the Sangreal at the battle, though the white knights could see it. Out of pride he regretted that he could not defeat the white, yet that was an earthly goal. He was on a heavenly Quest.

Gawain

Gawain was weary of the Quest, since he had been having even fewer adventures than usual. He met Sir Ector, Lancelot's brother. They slept and Gawain dreamed of bulls, black, white, and spotted. Ector dreamed of Lancelot in difficulty. They were sitting in a chapel discussing these dreams when they saw a vision of a hand and arm to the elbow, covered in red silk, with an ordinary bridle hung over it and a large candle grasped in the fist. The arm passed before them, went into the chapel, and disappeared.

In his search for adventure, Gawain jousted with a knight and fatally injured him. He was dismayed to find that the knight was another knight of the Round Table. A notice was put over the knight's tomb that he had been killed by Gawain.

Gawain and Ector went to a hermit who interpreted their dreams and vision. The black bulls were sinful (meaning sexual). The white were the pure: Galahad and Percivale. Bors was spotted, because he had had sex one time, but he had been redeemed. Lancelot in Ector's dream had been humbled and had recognized his sins. The hand in the vision was the Holy Ghost. The bridle was abstinence, and the candle was clearness of sight. The hermit told them that they did not have enough faith to attain the Grail.

Bors

Bors met a priest who heard his confession. The priest told him to eat only bread and water until he sat at the table with the Sangreal, and dressed him in a red coat.

Bors rode on and found a lady in a tower who needed his help. She offered him rich food, but he ate only bread and water. She offered herself, but he slept on the floor. As he slept, he dreamed of black and white birds. The next day Bors defeated the champion of her enemy and restored peace to the land.

A few days later in a forest he saw his brother Lionel being led along and beaten by thorn branches. Bors was preparing to save Lionel when a maiden was brought into the forest by a knight who intended to rape her. She called to Bors for help, and he was torn. Should he help her or save his brother?

Bors saved the maiden and took her to safety and came back to find his brother. He met a priest who told him that Lionel was dead and showed him the body. The priest also told Bors that he must give in to a woman who loved him or Lancelot would die and Bors would be blamed for his death and for the death of Lionel.

The priest took Bors to a tower where Bors met a woman who tried to seduce him. He blessed himself and the castle dissolved. Bors realized that he had seen fiends and made his way to an abbey. The abbot explained that Lionel was actually still alive and

that Bors was right to save the woman. She was worthy and Lionel was not. The dream of black and white birds was a warning that what is good may appear evil and what is evil may appear good. Evil is the old law.

Bors agreed to go to a tournament and met Lionel on the way. Lionel was furious that Bors had not saved him in the forest and left the woman to her fate. When Bors refused to fight him, Lionel rode over him with his horse and knocked him unconscious. He tried to cut off Bors' head, but a hermit ran out to stop him. Lionel killed the hermit. A knight of the Round Table came up and tried to save Bors, but Lionel killed him too. Bors came to and decided that he must fight Lionel after all, but he was saved from that when a flame and a cloud separated them. Bors rode away.

Galahad, Bors, Percivale, Percivale's Sister

Galahad was resting at a hermitage when a woman came for him. She took him to her mistress, who was the sister of Percivale. Percivale's sister took him to a ship covered with white silk, where Bors and Percivale were waiting for them.

On the ship there was a marvelous sword that, like the sword in the stone, could only be drawn by the greatest knight in the world. There were several stories about the sword, tracing it back to Joseph of Arimathea, and then even further back to King Solomon. Galahad claimed the sword.

The ship brought them to a castle where they were warned of danger. They were attacked and the three knights killed many people. Seeing what they had done, they wondered if they had sinned. A priest told them that they had not, since the people they had killed were evil and were not Christians. The king of the castle who had been imprisoned by the evil people came out and died in Galahad's arms.

During Mass they saw Jesus in a vision as a white hart. The priest told them this vision related to the virgin birth.

The group moved on, but as they passed one castle a knight came out and said if Percivale's sister was a virgin they could not pass unless she gave a bowlful of blood to heal the mistress of the castle. Galahad, Bors, and Percivale fought and killed several knights, but more came. Percivale's sister stopped them and said that she would give the blood to heal the woman. She gave the blood and healed the mistress of the castle. Too much blood was taken for her to live, though, and as she was dying she asked Percivale to put her body in a boat and she would meet them in the holy city of Sarras. They put her in their ship and went on by land.

Bors went on another adventure, while Galahad and Percivale explored the castle where Percivale's sister had died. They found the graves of many fair maidens, many daughters of kings, who had died giving blood. The next day all the people of the castle were struck down for their wickedness in killing the maidens.

Lancelot

Lancelot had a vision to enter the first ship he saw, and he boarded the ship where Percivale's sister was lying dead. He read of the adventures of the four and felt a great sweetness on the ship. He spent a month living there, fed on manna from heaven.

Galahad came and entered the ship with him. They spent six months together becoming acquainted as father and son, until a knight came to call Galahad back to the Quest. They parted, knowing they would never see each other again. Lancelot stayed for another month, praying to see tidings of the Sangreal.

He came to a castle where he heard beautiful music. He entered the castle and came to a chamber. The door of the chamber opened. He could not enter, but he saw the Grail covered in red silk on a table of silver, surrounded by candles. A man clothed as a priest appeared to be sacrificing the Mass. When the priest raised the host, Lancelot saw that he was really lifting a man and rushed in to help. Lancelot was knocked down by a breath of fire before he could get to the table and was carried away, looking as if he were dead.

Lancelot remained unconscious for twenty-four days, one day for every year of his sinfulness. When he woke, the people of the castle brought him new clothes, but he took the hair of the old man and put it next to his skin. They told him that the Sangreal had been achieved in him and that he would never attain more. King Pelles told him that Elaine was dead, and the Grail served them.

Ector came to the castle, but was denied entry. When he heard that Lancelot, his brother, was inside, he realized that it was true that he had been found unworthy. He rode off in shame. Lancelot was grieved to hear that Ector was unworthy to enter.

Lancelot returned to Camelot, seeing the tomb of the knight Gawain had killed on the way. When he returned he found that more than half of the Knights of the Round Table had been killed. Ector, Gawain, and Lionel and many others of the Quest had returned before him. He told them of his Quest and news of Galahad, Bors, and Percivale and his sister.

Galahad

Galahad came to King Mordrains who asked to die in his arms, and then he found the tomb of the knight Gawain had killed. Galahad was taken to a flaming tomb, where he found a relative who had dwelt in the flames for 300 years for a sin against Joseph of Arimathea. Galahad removed him from the flames, carried him to the church, and buried him there the next day.

Galahad rode on toward the Grail castle to see the Maimed King. He met Percivale and Bors and they rode to the castle of Carbonek. King Pelles and the people of the castle received them with great joy, since they had fulfilled the Quest for the Sangreal.

They were shown a broken sword that Percivale and Bors could not mend. Galahad put it together as though it had never been broken.

There was an announcement that the Grail was going to serve the worthy, so the others had to leave. Both Pelles and his son were forced to leave. Four women carried in a bed with a sick man with a crown of gold. This man had been waiting for Galahad to heal him. A man came from heaven dressed as a bishop, and letters on his forehead showed that he was Joseph of Arimathea. Angels came with candles, a towel, and a bleeding lance. Joseph raised bread in the air and they saw the image of a face enter the bread. Joseph put the bread in the Grail, kissed Galahad, and told him to kiss the others. Jesus, with the marks of the crucifixion, came out of the Grail and gave communion to all.

Jesus said that the Sangreal was the dish from which he ate the Passover lamb at the Last Supper. He told them that they would see the Grail more openly in the city of Sarras. They were to go there and take the Grail, for its guardians at the castle had failed to serve it properly. He also told Galahad to anoint the old king with blood from the lance. The king was healed, and they left the castle.

Sarras

In three days they came to a ship and found that the Grail was there. The ship sailed to Sarras, and when they arrived they found that the ship with the body of Percivale's sister had just arrived to meet them. As they went on land, Galahad healed a cripple, and they went to bury Percivale's sister.

The three told the king that they had come with the Grail, but the king was wicked and threw them in prison, where the Grail sustained them for a year. When the king died the people asked Galahad to be their king, and he agreed for a time. One year later he rose early to go to the Grail chapel. He found Joseph of Arimathea and angels there, saying Mass. Joseph invited Galahad to come forth and see what he has desired. When Galahad saw the vision, he wanted to die. After Joseph gave them communion, Galahad kissed Percivale and Bors and sent greetings to Lancelot. He died and angels carried his soul to heaven. A hand reached down from heaven and took the Grail, and it has never been seen in the world again.

After they buried Galahad next to Percivale's sister, Bors and Percivale went into the forest. Percivale became a hermit, and Bors stayed with him, though he did not become a religious. Percivale died one year and two months later, and Bors buried him with Galahad and his sister. Bors then went back to Camelot to bring them the news of the Grail Quest, and to give Galahad's message to Lancelot. The court rejoiced that the Quest had been achieved.

Reclaiming the Feminine Aspect of Christianity

We have already seen that the Grail stories are heretical under Church doctrine, but many have suggested that the true Grail story is even more heretical to a Church that has denied spiritual authority to women for almost two millennia. That is the story of the wife of Jesus. That story would have been serious heresy from the Church's point of view, and the experience of the Cathars would have been sufficient to convince people that the story could not be told directly. The story would have to be wrapped in such symbolism that only the initiated would understand its meaning.

A Hidden Tale:

The Chalice is a Woman

The canonical Gospels tell the story of the crucifixion, but none of them tell of streaming blood that was gathered in a vessel of some kind. Jesus is speared in the side, but is already dead and would not have bled much. What if the story of the gathering of the blood of Jesus is not a literal story about blood, but a story about blood in the sense of kinship? We call our family our flesh and blood, and we talk about descent in terms of bloodlines.

What if the vessel is not a cup or a chalice, but the living vessel of a woman's body? The chalice or cup was an ancient symbol of the female and of the womb.

This idea is heretical, because Church doctrine insists that both Mary the mother of Jesus and Jesus himself were perpetual virgins. The Church has made an extreme virtue of virginity, and many Christians feel so strongly about it that the movie, *The Last Temptation of Christ,* which portrayed Jesus as subject to sexual temptation, caused small riots.

Nonetheless, there is very little in the New Testament that would give us clues to the marital status of Jesus. Judaism has never favored celibacy, and Jesus was most definitely a Jew. Marriage and raising a family were generally considered important parts of living righteously as a Jew. Some Jewish groups of that time, such as the Essenes, were said to be celibate, but they lived in seclusion and tended to be legalistic in their interpretations of the Law. The Jesus of the New Testament traveled around with a group of disciples, including a sizeable group of women. He challenged legalistic interpretations of the law by defending his hungry disciples who picked food on the Sabbath and defending his right to heal on the Sabbath. He ate with people who others would have found unclean. He did not fit the profile of a member of any celibate group we know about.

Jesus was also called Rabbi at times in the New Testament. Generally, men were not allowed to be rabbis until they were married. So this title tends to indicate that he was married, as was expected of any Jewish man of his age. We have historical information about the criticism other groups made of Jesus. He was, of course, denounced as a criminal because of the crucifixion. The story of the virgin birth led to a charge that he was illegitimate, but there is no claim that he was unmarried, which is an accusation that might have been expected in that time and culture. An unmarried man was thought to be one who was not fulfilling his religious obligations. How could such a man be a religious leader? Yet this charge was never made against Jesus.

None of this proves that Jesus was married, but it shows that the possibility is not at all farfetched. If Jesus was married, who was his wife? The most likely candidate is the woman who legend says caught his blood in a cup or in a basket of eggs. In this context, both stories take on a significant symbolism of the womb and fertility. That woman is Mary Magdalene.

Mary Magdalene
and the Holy Blood

Many people in the West do not think Mary Magdalene is a likely wife for Jesus, because she was portrayed by the Western Church as a prostitute and praised as a repentant sinner. Pope Gregory made this the official portrait of Mary Magdalene in the sixth century. It is unclear whether he was relying on earlier theories or creating his own, but his assertions have no valid basis in the New Testament. The Catholic Church acknowledged this in 1969, and left open the question of what the role of Mary Magdalene really was.

The first three Gospels portray her as the leader of the women at the crucifixion, and Mark and Matthew show her as the first witness to the resurrection and the messenger to the other apostles. In the Gospel of John Mary is part of a family party, as she stands at the foot of the cross with the beloved disciple and the mother and aunt of Jesus. She is again the witness to the resurrection.

In apocryphal texts Mary Magdalene is portrayed as the companion of Jesus, as the woman Jesus loved more than the other disciples, and the woman he kissed. Some

argue that this kissing was purely symbolic and mystical, but it may not have been. She is also portrayed as the disciple who understood the teachings of Jesus best and who was the best teacher of others. She comforts the other disciples after the death of Jesus and encourages them to spread the word.

In these texts she is called, "the woman who knew All," "the woman who revealed the greatness of the revealer," "the one who is the inheritor of the light," and "the apostle who excels the rest."

All of this indicates that Mary Magdalene may well have been the wife of Jesus and/or one of his leading disciples and apostles. From the dating of the apocryphal texts, it is very likely that a tradition teaching about Mary Magdalene existed in the early second century and quite possibly in the first century.

In the earliest versions of Christianity Mary Magdalene, not Mary the mother of Jesus, was the most important woman around Jesus. The Eastern Church was instrumental in helping to replace Mary Magdalene with Mary the Mother, even changing some apocryphal texts to make Mary the mother of Jesus appear to be the Mary at the tomb and the witness to the resurrection. In spite of this, the Eastern Church never vilified Mary Magdalene as a prostitute, as the Western Church did for 15 centuries.

The Eastern Church has two legends about Mary Magdalene and eggs. One, which we already mentioned, was that she stood at the foot of the cross and caught the blood of Jesus in a basket of eggs that turned red. Another is that she went to Rome with Mary the mother of Jesus and appeared before the emperor Tiberius. When Mary Magdalene told him the story of the resurrection of Jesus he jeered and said that a man could no more rise from the dead than an egg could turn red. In response, Mary Magdalene picked up an egg and it instantly turned bright red.

Another legend blossomed in France just before the crusades, and just before the Grail stories began to appear. That legend said that after the crucifixion Mary Magdalene was driven out of the Holy Land and placed in a ship without oars at sea. Miraculously, that ship brought her safely to Marseilles. In the legend she is said to have converted the people and then gone into a contemplative retirement. Finding her body became a common quest in the Middle Ages, and with the usual overindulgence of the time, about six of her bodies were "found."

There is another legend, probably related to the Gospel of John, that Mary Magdalene went to Ephesus to live with Mary the mother of Jesus and became a recluse there. If there is any truth in these legends, it is possible that she went first to Ephesus and then to Marseilles, where she eventually entered a life of contemplation.

The Abbey Church of St. Marie-Madeleine at Vézelay was begun in 1096 and completed in the mid 1100s, a few decades before the first Grail story was written. This shrine to Mary Magdalene was the most important pilgrimage center in France at the time and the fourth most important pilgrimage site in Christendom, after Jerusalem, Rome, and Compostela, in Santiago, Spain, where legend says the body of St. James is buried.

One theory is that the Cathars held the secret of Mary Magdalene and it was because of the flowering of their culture that stories of her became more common. Their respect for the feminine in religion and the troubadour's tributes to the Lady, might have been in reverence of Mary Magdalene. If the Cathars held information that contradicted orthodox Christian doctrine, the Church's extreme violence toward them is more understandable. The stories of the troubadours that were influenced by Cathar culture became an important component of the Grail legend, as did the story that the blood of Jesus was brought to Europe in a sacred vessel.

If the legend that the secrets of the Cathars were preserved is true, what happened to them? One possibility is that they were entrusted to the Cathars' allies, the Knights Templar. Quite a few French Templars were from Cathar families, and their ties to the Cathar community were strong. If the Cathars were looking for a group powerful enough to protect their secrets and treasure, the Knights Templar were the most likely choice.

The Knights Templar themselves are often believed to have had secrets of their own. The theory is that Bernard of Clairvaux and the Count of Champagne discovered that something important was buried under the Temple in Jerusalem. They used their influence to have both the Order of Sion and the Knights Templar established in Jerusalem with access to the Temple Mount. Part of what they found there may have been information about the life of Jesus and his relationship with Mary Magdalene. We know from the discovery of the Dead Sea Scrolls that some Jewish texts were hidden before the war with Rome in the first century, so it would not be surprising if the Templars found some.

If the Knights Templar had information that threatened the Church, that might account for both their meteoric rise to power and wealth and their sudden destruction. Historical accounts are clear that the Templars in France made away with both their treasury and their fleet of ships and that neither were ever captured by the Church. A popular theory is that the fleet sailed to Templar holdings in Ireland and then Scotland. Scotland was a likely choice, because the king of the time, Bruce, was at odds with the Church and had been excommunicated. He was not likely to take orders from the Vatican and might have welcomed the Vatican's enemies.

If the Templar treasure, and perhaps the Cathar treasure, went to Scotland, what happened to them after that? One Scottish group has long claimed to be based on the Templars: the Freemasons. The Freemasons were originally an artisans guild for builders, but a form of speculative Freemasonry evolved that include interest in ancient and occult subjects that seemed to have interested the Templars as well.

There is a very interesting chapel in Scotland, called Rosslyn Chapel, that has long interested Grail researchers. This purports to be a Christian church, but is filled with pagan imagery. It is full of intricate masonry work and is the source of a Freemason legend about a master mason who killed an apprentice in jealousy over the work of the apprentice. Many believe that the Templar treasure and the Templar secrets were buried there at least at one time.

The Conspiracey Continues?

A nother twist to the Mary Magdalene Grail story is the belief that the descendents of Jesus and Mary Magdalene may have intermarried with the Merovingian royal line in France. The last official Merovingian king was Dagobert II, who was murdered in 679. The French throne was later usurped by the Carolingians. As a result, the Mary Magdalene story has become intertwined with the story of bloodlines or royal blood, the Sang Real.

That the story of Mary Magdalene is sometimes mixed with advocacy for return of the Merovingian dynasty is somewhat ironic. The Carolingian rulers married Merovingian princesses, and the bloodline continued in the royal house. The controversy is based on a belief that the male bloodline is more important than the female bloodline, and that descendents of male Meroviangians have more right to rule than descendents of female Merovingians.

The story of the bloodlines has been fueled by the discovery of a group of documents called the *Dossiers Secrets* in France's Bibliothèque Nationale, where they were deposited in 1956. These documents claim that the Order of Sion has continued to the present as a nonreligious order called the Priory of Sion, and that this group is the holder of the Templar secrets. The documents also list past grand masters of the Priory of Sion. The list includes several women grand masters in the early centuries, though not in recent times. The list of grand masters includes some of the most famous men of their times, such as Leonard da Vinci, Robert Fludd, Issac Newton, and Victor Hugo.

Leonardo da Vinci is probably the most interesting figure listed, because at least one of his paintings is said to present a unique view of Mary Magdalene. His fifteenth-century painting of tempera and oil on plaster in the Convent of Santa Maria delle Grazie in Milan has been restored many times over the centuries. When it was recently restored again, the clumsy efforts of past restorers were removed, revealing a very feminine figure sitting on the right side of Jesus. Art experts claim this is John, who was often portrayed as a beautiful and feminine young man in Italian art. Others believe that it is a portrait of Mary Magdalene, seated at the side of Jesus.

In the painting Peter leans toward the feminine figure with a possibly unfriendly expression on his face. Behind him a hand—that some have claimed is disembodied—holds a dagger. Art experts say that the arm belongs to Peter, and a close view of the painting shows that the hand is Peter's held at an odd angle, as though he is trying to hide the knife. This can be more clearly seen in the copy of Leonardo's painting by Marco d'Oggiono c. 1530.

The arm with a dagger has been explained as a representation of Peter drawing a sword when the Roman soldiers came to arrest Jesus, but that arrest took place in the Garden of Gethsemane, not at the Last Supper. On the other hand, Leonardo has Judas clutching his bag of silver, so the knife might represent the sword drawn in the garden. Yet that is not the only possible explanation.

Apocryphal texts about Mary Magdalene discovered in the twentieth century provide another explanation. In those texts Peter is portrayed as an adversary of Mary Magdalene, jealous of her relationship with Jesus and resentful of her position as a leading apostle. Mary Magdalene describes him as a threat to all women and says that she is afraid of him. Combined with the legend that Mary Magdalene was forced to flee the Holy Land, this portrayal of Peter raises interesting questions.

These texts were not discovered until centuries after Leonardo lived, but if he really was a member of an organization with access to the Cathar or Templar information or to Gnostic groups that preserved the tradition about Mary Magdalene and Peter, that might explain Peter's apparently threatening visage and the dagger that might be meant for the feminine figure.

If Leonardo intended to convey a secret message in this painting, as some believe he did, he could not have safely made this portrayal too obviously heretical, so it is not surprising that art experts would be able to vehemently defend the orthodoxy of the painting and explain away its odd features. Everyone will judge for themselves what Leonardo intended. Was this a subtle communication about the role of Mary Magdalene and the threat that Peter and other male apostles posed to her and to Christian women in general?

On the other hand, there is little historical evidence to support the Priory of Sion's claim that it is the continuation of the ancient Order of Sion. The list of past masters in the *Dossiers Secretes* begins with the same eight names as on an old Freemason list of secret Templar Grand Masters, and may be just a continuation of that list. We do not know if Leonardo was really associated with the Freemasons or the Priory of Sion, or if he was interested in Mary Magdalen or Merovingian bloodlines.

The Grail Quest Today

oday the Grail Quest takes different forms for different people. It's the quest to unravel a mystery and find out what really happened, a quest to discover historical truth, and a quest to reclaim the feminine aspect of Christianity. It's the quest to rediscover a bloodline and facilitate the Return of the King. For the few claiming that bloodline, it may be a quest for power.

For others the quest is not about history. It is the archetypal journey of Perceval toward greater compassion and understanding. It is a quest for mystical union and for the sacred in our very secular world. This is a quest for the ultimate source and the meaning of life.

Acknowledgments

Angelika Engelhardt-Rotthaus, Bingen, 81; Archivo Scala, Florence, 126; Art Resource, 34; Arthur Rackham, 44, 68, 98, 103; Bibliotheca Real, Madrid, 28; Bibliotheque de l'Arsenal, Paris, 116; Bibliotheque Nationale, Paris, 47, 108, 113, 139; Bildarchiv Preussischer Kulturbesitz, Berlin, 14; Birmingham City Museums & Art Gallery, Birmingham, 82, 107, 119; Bodlien Library, Oxford, 111; Bridgeman Art Library, London, 27; British Library, London, 32, 59, 73, 93; British Museum, London, 40; Chateau d'Ecouen, 147; Church of San Vitale, Ravenna, 19; Collezione Isabela Far De Chirico, Rome, 125; Dante Rossetti, 76; Gallerie dell'Academia, Florence, 128; Holy Transfiguration Monastery, Brookline, MA, 135; Hubert Josse, Paris, 20; Kunsthistorisches Museum, Vienna, 8; Louis Rhead, 54, 67, 75, 88, 94, 96, 104; M.L. Kirk, 11; Manchester City Art Galleries, 122; Mary Evans Picture Library, London, 22, 85; Musee Jaquemart-Andre, France, 150; National Gallery of Scotland, Edinburgh, 142; National Gallery, London, 136; National Geographic, 17, 24; National Museum of Ireland, 63; National Trust, England, 114; Osterreichische Nationalbibliothek, Vienna, Austria, 90; Parish of St. Godehard, Hildesheim, Germany, 132; Rosslyn Chapel, Scotland, 141; Scala, Florence, 33; Stifsbibliothek in Kremsmunster, 6; Tate Gallery, London, Cover, 76; Tretyakov Gallery, Moscow, 53; Uffizi Gallery, Florence, 130, 148; Universitatbibliothek Heidelberg, 12, 71, 86;Weitzmann Schatzkammer Munchen, 50.